STARFISH

by **Mari Schuh**

D1324044

Raintree is an imprint of Capstone Global Library Limited, a company incorporated in England and Wales having its registered office at 7 Pilgrim Street, London, EC4V 6LB – Registered company number: 6695582

www.raintree.co.uk
myorders@raintree.co.uk

Editorial Credits
Elizabeth R. Johnson, editor; Aruna Rangarajan, designer;
Kelly Garvin, media researcher; Tori Abraham, production specialist

ISBN 978 1 4747 0480 9 (hardcover)
19 18 17 16 15
10 9 8 7 6 5 4 3 2 1

ISBN 978 1 4747 0485 4 (paperback)
20 19 18 17 16
10 9 8 7 6 5 4 3 2 1

British Library Cataloguing in Publication Data
A full catalogue record for this book is available from the British Library.

Photo Credits
Newscom/Gordon MacSkimming/PictureNature/Photoshot, 19; SeaPics.com: Andrew J. Martinez, 17, Celeste Fowler, 11, Doug Perrine, 15, Tim Hellier, 21; Shutterstock: Andrea Izzotti, cover, 9, 13, Godruma, cover (background), Longjourneys, 7, Vilainecrevette, 5

Design Elements: Shutterstock: Kasia, SusIO, Vectomart

Printed and bound in China.

Contents

Life in the sea

Starfish crawl on the seabed.
These colourful animals look
for food to eat.

Starfish live in seas and oceans around the world. There are about 1,500 types of starfish. They are found in both shallow and deep water.

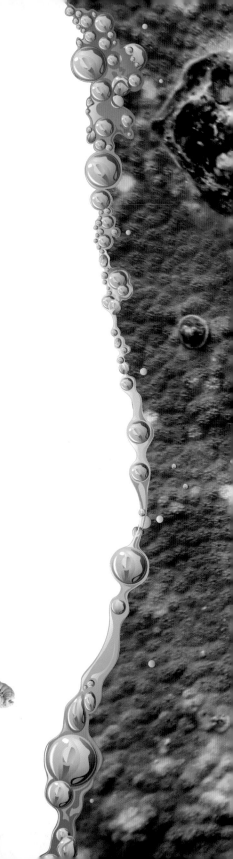

Up close

Most starfish have five arms.
Some have 40 arms!
If a starfish loses an arm,
it can grow a new one.

Starfish can be many sizes.
Some are less than
2.5 centimetres wide.
Others grow to be more
than 1 metre wide.

Starfish have tough skin
on their thick arms.
Short spines protect
starfish from predators.

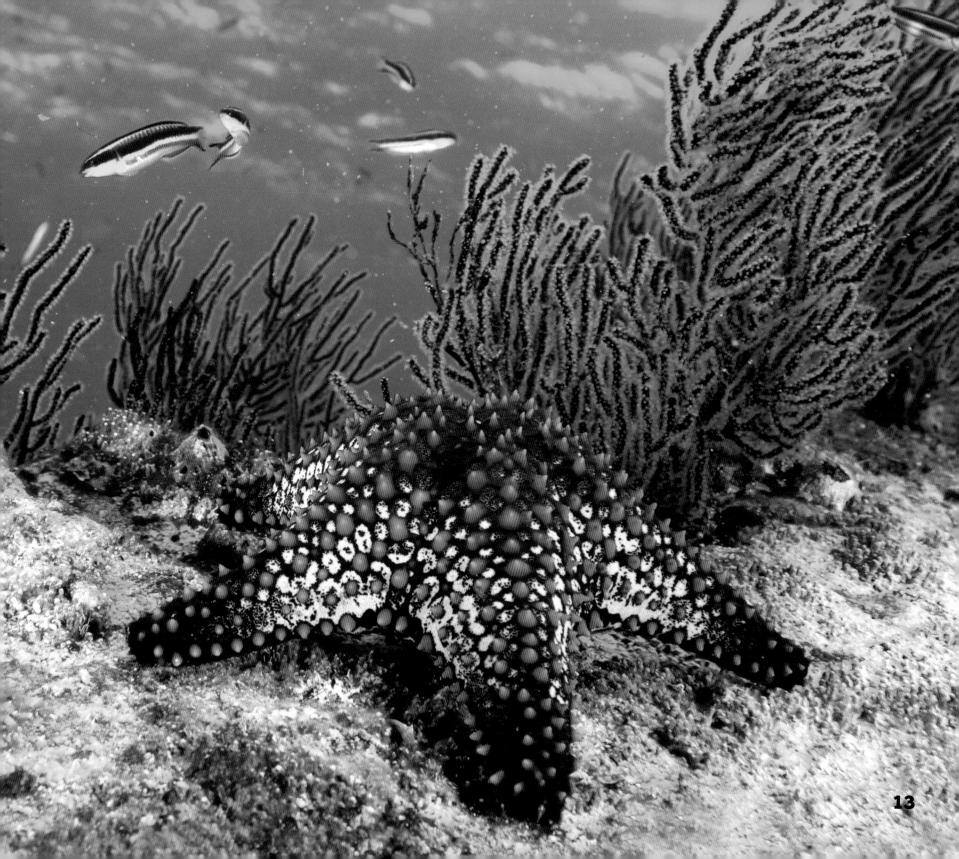

Starfish have hundreds of tiny tube feet. Their feet help them to crawl on coral reefs and rocky shores. Their feet grab prey, too.

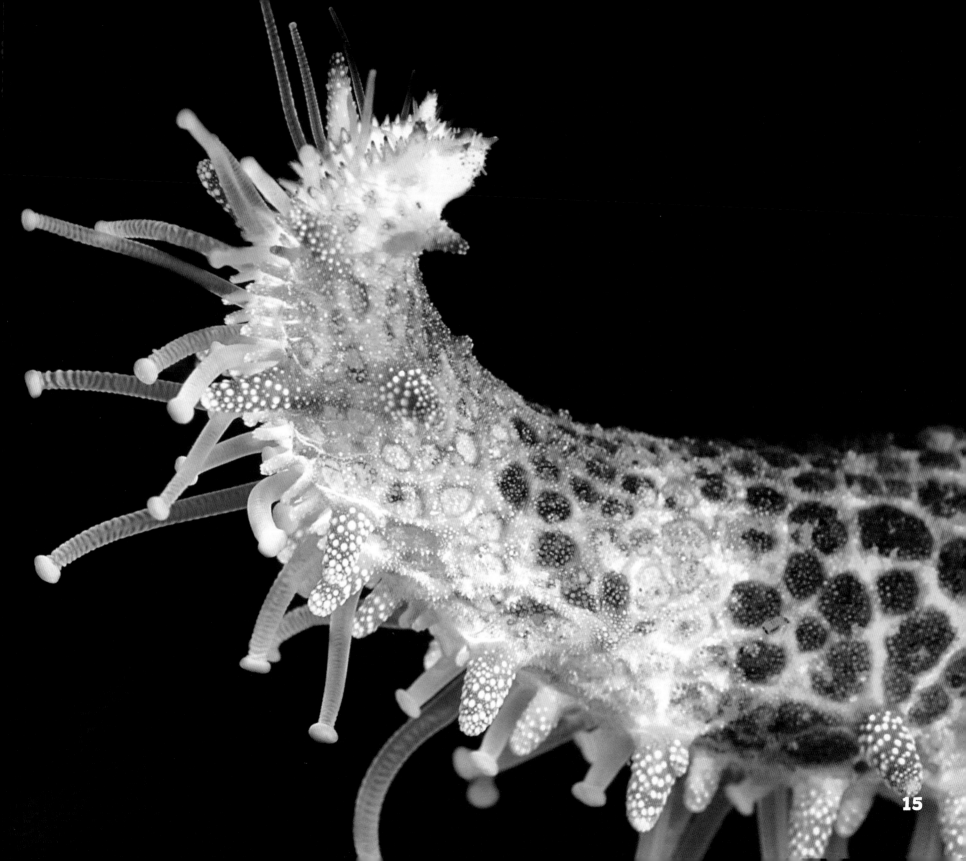

Finding food

Starfish open clam shells with their feet. They push their stomachs outside their bodies. They stick their stomachs inside the clam shells. Then starfish eat their prey.

Life cycle

Some female starfish
lay thousands of eggs.
Male starfish put sperm into
the water. When the eggs
and sperm meet,
the eggs are fertilized.

The fertilized eggs grow
into tiny larvae.
The larvae float in the sea
for up to 45 days.
Then they grow into
starfish on the seabed.

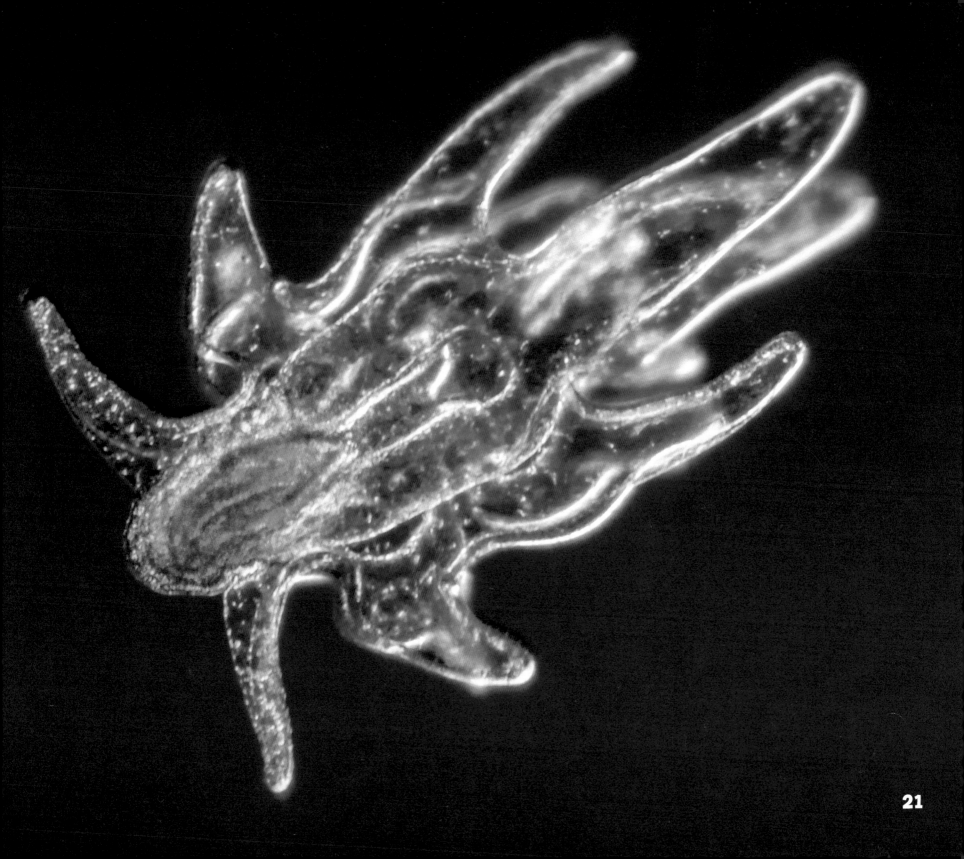

Glossary

coral reef type of land close to the surface of the sea made up of the hardened bodies of corals; corals are small, colourful sea creatures

fertilize join an egg of a female with a sperm of a male to produce young

larva animal at the stage of development between an egg and an adult; more than one larva are larvae

predator animal that hunts other animals for food

prey animal hunted by another animal for food

protect guard or keep something safe from harm

shallow not deep

sperm one of the reproductive cells from a male that can fertilize the eggs of a female

spine hard, sharp, pointed growth on an animal's body

Read more

Fish Body Parts (Animal Body Parts), Clare Lewis (Raintree, 2015)

Sea Animals (Animals in their Habitats), Sian Smith (Raintree, 2014)

Usborne First Encyclopedia of Seas and Oceans, Jane Chisholm (Usborne Publishing, 2011)

Websites

www.bbc.co.uk/nature/life/Sunflower_starfish
Find out about the sunflower starfish.

www.national-aquarium.co.uk/50-fun-facts
Fun facts about sea and ocean life.

Index